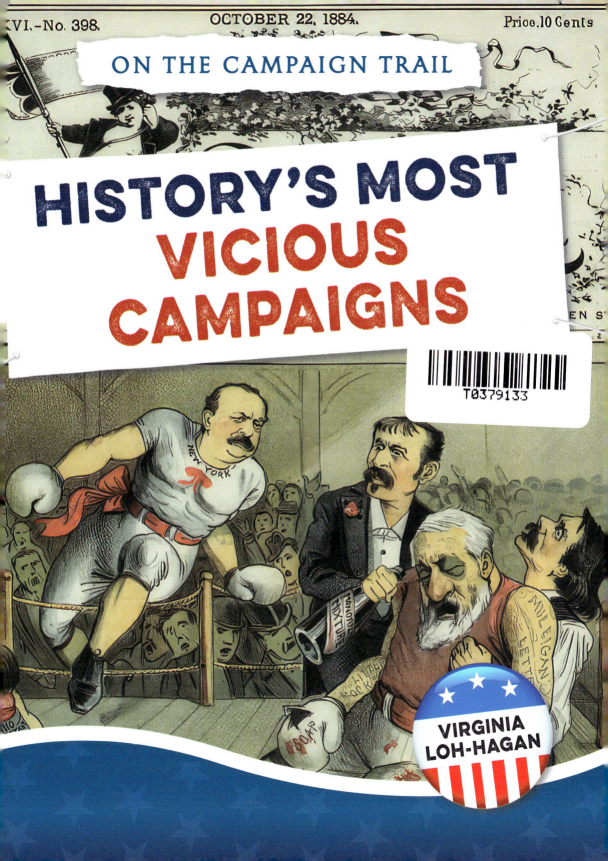

Published in the United States of America by Cherry Lake Publishing Group
Ann Arbor, Michigan
www.cherrylakepublishing.com

Reading Adviser: Beth Walker Gambro, MS, Ed., Reading Consultant, Yorkville, IL
Content Adviser: Mark Richards, Ph.D., Professor, Dept. of Political Science, Grand Valley State University, Allendale, MI
Book Designer: Frame25 Productions

Photo Credits: Prints and Photographs Division, Library of Congress, cover, title page; © Allison C Bailey/Shutterstock, 5; © New Africa/Shutterstock, 7; Rembrandt Peale, Public domain, via Wikimedia Commons, 9; John Trumbull, Public domain, via Wikimedia Commons, 9; Alexander Gardner, Public domain, via Wikimedia Commons, 13; University of Texas, Public domain, via Wikimedia Commons, 17; Euthman Ed Uthman, CC BY-SA 3.0 via Wikimedia Commons, 19; Office of Senator John McCain, Public domain, via Wikimedia Commons, 21; © Rebekah Zemansky/Shutterstock, 27; © Krakenimages.com/Shutterstock, 29; © Grindstone Media Group/Shutterstock, 31

Copyright © 2025 by Cherry Lake Publishing Group

All rights reserved. No part of this book may be reproduced or utilized in any form or by any means without written permission from the publisher.

45th Parallel Press is an imprint of Cherry Lake Publishing Group.

Library of Congress Cataloging-in-Publication Data has been filed and is available at catalog.loc.gov

Cherry Lake Publishing Group would like to acknowledge the work of the Partnership for 21st Century Learning, a Network of Battelle for Kids. Please visit Battelle for Kids online for more information.

Note from publisher: Websites change regularly, and their future contents are outside of our control. Supervise children when conducting any recommended online searches for extended learning opportunities.

Printed in the United States of America

ABOUT THE AUTHOR

Dr. Virginia Loh-Hagan is an author and educator. She is currently the Director of the Asian Pacific Islander Desi American (APIDA) Center at San Diego State University and the Co-Executive Director of The Asian American Education Project. She lives in San Diego with her very tall husband and very naughty dogs.

CONTENTS

Introduction 4

Chapter 1: **Fighting Founding Fathers (1796 and 1800)** . . 8

Chapter 2: **Battle for Public Opinion (1828)** 10

Chapter 3: **Honest Abe vs. Little Giant (1858)** 12

Chapter 4: **Private Made Public (1884)** 14

Chapter 5: **Too Close for Comfort (1948)** 16

Chapter 6: **A Fake Letter (1972)** 18

Chapter 7: **Rumors (2000)** 20

Chapter 8: **Attack Ads (2008)** 22

Chapter 9: **Stalking and Slashing (2012)** 24

Chapter 10: **Name-Calling (2016)** 26

Do Your Part! 28

Glossary, Learn More, Index 32

INTRODUCTION

The United States is a top world power. It's not ruled by kings or queens. It's a **democracy**. A democracy is a system of government. It means "rule by the people." People **elect** their leaders. They choose leaders by voting.

Leaders **represent** the people who voted for them. They speak for them. They make decisions for them. That's why voting is so important. By voting, we choose our leaders.

Candidates run for **public office**. Public office is a government position. Candidates work hard to get votes. They run **campaigns**. They do this before an election. Campaigns are planned activities. Some campaigns are easy. Some are hard. And some are full of drama.

In a democracy, people vote for their leaders. But they still speak out when they don't agree with how leaders run things.

Candidates run against other candidates. They compete for one position. They need to get the most votes. They have to beat the other candidates. This is how they win.

Some candidates run fair campaigns. Some don't. Their campaigns are **vicious**. Vicious means cruel. Some candidates attack others. They say mean things. They focus on negatives. They make their **opponents** look bad. Opponents are the competition.

Candidates should be role models. But competitions change people. Some people will do anything to win. There have been many vicious campaigns in U.S. history. This book features some of the most interesting ones!

Some candidates run unopposed. They're the only person running in an election.

CHAPTER ONE

FIGHTING FOUNDING FATHERS
(1796 AND 1800)

John Adams (1735–1826) was the 2nd U.S. president. Thomas Jefferson (1743–1826) was the 3rd U.S. president. Sometimes they were friends. Sometimes they were enemies. They had different ideas about government. Adams favored a strong central government. Jefferson favored states' rights.

In 1796 and 1800, they both ran for president. Their fans said mean things about the opposition. Jefferson's fans made fun of Adams. They called him a fool. They called him a criminal. They called him fat. They accused him of wanting to be a king. Adams's fans made fun of Jefferson's family. They called him a coward. They called him weak.

Jefferson and Adams became friends later. They wrote letters to each other.

John Adams and Thomas Jefferson died on the same day. They died on July 4, 1826.

CHAPTER TWO

BATTLE FOR PUBLIC OPINION (1828)

John Quincy Adams (1767–1848) was the 6th U.S. president. Andrew Jackson (1767–1845) was the 7th U.S. president. They ran against each other in 1828. This has been called the most vicious campaign. Both candidates' fans made many personal attacks.

Jackson was a war hero. He was popular. Adams's fans called him a murderer. They said he was violent. They said he was a cheater.

Jackson's fans fought back. They accused Adams of being **corrupt**. Corrupt means dishonest. They said Adams misused money. They said he was a snob. They said he abused women. Jackson won. Adams refused to go to his victory party.

WORLD AFFAIRS

Other countries have had vicious campaigns. Vladimir Lenin (1870–1924) was a Soviet Union leader. The Soviet Union was a national union of 15 countries. Russia was the largest country. Lenin led the Bolshevik Party. The Bolsheviks are a communist political party. They seized power in 1917. Lenin died in 1924.

This led to chaos. Joseph Stalin (1878–1953) saw his chance. He fought for power. He made statements against Lenin. He pushed his own ideas. He declared himself dictator in 1929. Dictator means supreme leader. Stalin made friends with the secret police. He put his friends in power. He promoted anyone loyal to him. He got rid of anyone against him. Stalin started the Great Terror in 1934. He killed a popular Bolshevik leader. He killed more. He jailed others. He purged the country of Bolsheviks. The Soviet Union later broke apart in 1991.

CHAPTER THREE

HONEST ABE vs. LITTLE GIANT
(1858)

In 1858, Stephen Douglas (1813–1861) was famous. Abraham Lincoln (1809–1865) was not. They both ran for U.S. senator in Illinois.

Douglas and Lincoln traveled all over Illinois. They went to 7 cities. They did 7 **debates**. Debates are formal arguments. Douglas and Lincoln mainly talked about slavery. Douglas called Lincoln "dangerous." Lincoln said Douglas's thinking was **immoral**. Immoral means sinful or wrong.

Douglas was elected senator. But in 1860, Douglas and Lincoln ran for U.S. president. Candidates from 2 other political parties also ran. Lincoln won the election.

The Lincoln-Douglas debates were each 3 hours long. Lincoln didn't win the 1858 Illinois senate seat. But he became president in 1860.

CHAPTER FOUR
PRIVATE MADE PUBLIC
(1884)

In 1884, Grover Cleveland (1837–1908) ran for U.S. president. He beat James G. Blaine (1830–1893). But it wasn't easy.

A newspaper shared Cleveland's private life. It said Cleveland had a child with a woman who was not his wife. Blaine's fans chanted, "Ma, ma! Where's my pa?"

Cleveland's fans called Blaine the "liar from Maine." Blaine had many scandals. Some people stopped believing in him. They thought he was corrupt. They switched their votes to Cleveland. Their votes helped Cleveland win.

THE IDEAL CANDIDATE

Ideal candidates are role models. Shirley Chisholm (1924–2005) was the first Black woman elected to Congress. She was also the first to run for U.S. president. This was in 1972. Chisholm ran a clean campaign. Her slogan was "unbought and unbossed." She had a lot of experience. She served in local, state, and national government. She fought for education. She fought for school lunches. She fought for food stamps. She fought for women and people of color. Still, she faced a lot of hate. She had to fight racism. She didn't get much media coverage. She only made one speech on TV. She was criticized for being Black and a woman. But she focused on her ideas. She paved the way for others. She said, "I want to be remembered as a catalyst for change in America." Catalyst means something that speeds up change.

CHAPTER FIVE

TOO CLOSE FOR COMFORT
(1948)

In 1948, there was a Senate race. This race took place in Texas. Lyndon B. Johnson (1908–1973) was a candidate. So was Coke Stevenson (1888–1975).

On election day, Johnson seemed to be losing. Six days later, 203 votes were added. 202 votes were for Johnson. One vote was for Stevenson. This put Johnson in the lead. The votes were recounted. Johnson won by 87 votes. Many thought this was too close.

Stevenson accused Johnson of **fraud**. Fraud means lying or cheating. Johnson fought back. He denied fraud. He told Stevenson to produce proof. Stevenson asked for an investigation. He took the case to court. Johnson won. But many accused him of stealing the election.

Coke Stevenson had a reason to fight back. The added names were in alphabetical order. They were written with the same pen. They had the same handwriting.

CHAPTER SIX
A FAKE LETTER
(1972)

Edmund Muskie (1914–1996) ran for U.S. president. He did this in 1972. He wanted to be the Democratic Party's candidate.

The *Union Leader* is a New Hampshire newspaper. It published a handwritten letter. It was signed by "Paul Morrison." Morrison said he met Muskie at a campaign event. He said Muskie's staff made racist remarks. He said Muskie laughed. Newspapers said Muskie was a bad person. They also said his wife drank, smoked, and cursed. George McGovern was named the Democratic candidate instead of Muskie. Richard Nixon (1913–1994) was the Republican Party's candidate.

The letter that started it all was fake. It was written by Nixon's staff members. Even so, Nixon won the election.

Muskie was very upset by the *Union Leader* letter.
People said he cried about it. He denied it.

CHAPTER SEVEN
RUMORS
(2000)

John McCain (1936–2018) fought in the Vietnam War (1954–1975). He was a prisoner of war. He campaigned as a war hero. But his biggest battle took place in South Carolina. It was the Republican primary. McCain was running to be the Republican candidate for president. He ran against George W. Bush (born 1946). This took place in 2000.

Push polls are used in dirty politics. They don't collect opinions. They sway voters. Push polls spread nasty rumors about McCain. They suggested McCain had fathered a child outside of his marriage. Bush won the nomination. He also was elected president.

John McCain won the Republican nomination in 2008. But he lost the election to Democrat Barack Obama (born 1961).

CHAPTER EIGHT
ATTACK ADS
(2008)

The 2008 Senate race in North Carolina got nasty. It's one of the meanest campaigns. Kay Hagan (1953–2019) ran against Elizabeth Dole (born 1936).

Dole was expected to win. But Hagan was good at raising money. This made Dole nervous. Dole attacked Hagan. She ran ads. The ads questioned Hagan's faith. They said she hung out with "godless Americans." They said she accepted "godless" money. They showed a photo of Hagan. A voice said, "There is no God."

Hagan sued Dole. She attacked Dole. She also defended herself. She said she taught Sunday school at her church. She won. But it was a close election.

HOT-BUTTON ISSUE

Hot-button issues refer to tough topics. People have strong emotions. They take sides. They like some candidates. They hate others. In vicious campaigns, candidates attack each other. It's hard to know what's true. People need proof. They use pictures as proof. They use videos as proof. They use audio as proof. But today, these things can be faked. People use technology. They make deepfakes. Deepfakes are dirty tricks. People change videos. They change pictures. They change sound. They use deepfakes to destroy candidates. They show candidates saying or doing things they're not doing. There is a well-known altered video of Nancy Pelosi (born 1940). Pelosi was the Speaker of the House of Representatives. She was in charge of Congress. This video made her look drunk. It was viewed more than 2 million times. It made her look bad. Altered videos confuse voters. No one knows what's true or not. They sway votes based on lies.

CHAPTER NINE
STALKING AND SLASHING (2012)

Gary Smith ran for Congress in 2012. He wanted to represent New Mexico. He ran against Janice Arnold-Jones (born 1952). Arnold-Jones was far ahead.

Arnold-Jones complained about Smith. Candidates must get voters' signatures to run for office. Some of Smith's signatures were not valid. Smith was kicked out of the race. He got mad. He stalked Arnold-Jones. He slashed her tires. Arnold-Jones had him on camera.

Smith slashed other people's tires. He was sent to jail. Arnold-Jones said, "He's been warned to not come near any of us."

FACT-CHECK

It's important to check facts. Facts must be correct. Here are some fun facts about vicious campaigns:

- Upton Sinclair (1878–1968) was a writer. He wrote a book about the meat-packing business. He exposed many issues. He ran for California governor. Businessmen across the country united. They raised money to defeat him. Newspapers attacked him. Newsreels showed negative ads. Sinclair lost the election.

- Walter Mondale (1928–2021) ran for U.S. president in 1984. He ran against Ronald Reagan (1911–2004). Mondale made attack ads. He said voting for Reagan meant nuclear war. He said Reagan broke his campaign promises. He said, "He forgot you. And now it's your turn to forget him…" Reagan was popular. He said life improved under his leadership. His slogan was, "It's morning again in America." He won by a landslide. Landslide means winning most of the votes.

CHAPTER TEN
NAME-CALLING (2016)

The 2016 U.S. presidential election was full of name-calling. Republican Donald Trump (born 1946) and Democrat Hillary Clinton (born 1947) ran against each other.

Trump called Clinton many names. He called her "Crooked Hillary." He called her "crazy" and a "nasty woman." He said she was a liar. His supporters spread rumors about her. They said she was sick. They said she killed opponents. They said she had a body double.

Clinton accused Trump of spreading "racist lies." Clinton called Trump's supporters "racists" and "haters." She called them "**deplorables**." Deplorables means shameful people. This comment shifted some voters toward Trump. He won the election.

Hillary Clinton won the popular vote in 2016 but lost the electoral vote. Donald Trump won the presidency.

DO YOUR PART!

U.S. citizens have 2 special rights. Only U.S. citizens can vote in federal elections. Only U.S. citizens can run for **federal office**. Federal office means a national office. It's different from state and local offices.

U.S. citizens have many other rights. But they also have duties. The most powerful is the duty to vote. Voting is how people choose leaders. It's how people make changes. It's how people promote their ideas. Those elected make the laws. They make policies. They make the rules. They work for voters.

U.S. citizens can vote at age 18. But people are never too young to get involved in democracy.

Election day for federal elections occurs between November 2 and November 8.

Citizens should be kind to others. They should choose candidates with good **character**. Character is the way someone thinks, feels, and acts. It matters. Here are things to think about when voting:

★ Listen to how candidates talk about other candidates. See if they're respectful. See if they're team players.

★ Learn about the candidates' ideas. Find out what they stand for. Make sure you believe in the same things.

★ Pay attention to how candidates treat voters. See if they listen to voters' issues.

Everyone can do their part. Being a good citizen is hard work. But the work is worth it. Your vote is your voice.

Good candidates have a clear message. Messages are important.

GLOSSARY

campaigns (kam-PAYNZ) organized courses of action to achieve a goal such as winning an election

candidates (KAN-duh-dayts) people who want to be elected to certain positions

character (KAIR-ik-tur) the way someone thinks, feels, and behaves

corrupt (kuh-RUHPT) dishonest, immoral

debates (dih-BAYTS) formal discussions between two people or groups with opposing views

democracy (dih-MAH-kruh-see) a system of government led by elected representatives

deplorables (dih-PLOR-uh-buhlz) shameful, dishonorable people

elect (ih-LEKT) to choose someone to hold public office by voting

federal office (FEH-druhl AW-fuhs) an elected position in the national government

fraud (FRAWD) false representation of facts by lying, cheating, or trickery

immoral (ih-MOHR-uhl) unethical, wrongful, or evil

opponents (uh-POH-nuhnts) people who are competing against other people

public office (PUH-blik AW-fuhs) government position established by law

push polls (PUSH POHLZ) a negative campaigning technique that sways voters by putting ideas into their heads while asking their opinions

represent (reh-prih-ZENT) to speak or act for another person or group

vicious (VIH-shuhs) cruel or violent

LEARN MORE

Books

Berne, Emma Carlson. *Election Campaigns: A Kid's Guide*. North Mankato, MN: Capstone Press, 2020.

Cunningham, Kevin. *How Political Campaigns and Elections Work*. Minneapolis: ABDO Publishing, 2015.

Yacka, Douglas. *What Is a Presidential Election?* New York: Penguin Workshop, 2020.

INDEX

Adams, John, 8–9
Adams, John Quincy, 10
Arnold-Jones, Janice, 24

Blaine, James G., 14
Bush, George W., 20

candidates, 4, 6–7, 30–31
character, 6, 30
Chisholm, Shirley, 15
Cleveland, Grover, 14
Clinton, Hillary, 26–27
congressional elections, 12, 15, 16–17, 22, 24

debates, 12–13
deepfakes, 23
Dole, Elizabeth, 22
Douglas, Stephen, 12–13

fraud, 16–17, 18, 23, 24

Hagan, Kay, 22

Jackson, Andrew, 10
Jefferson, Thomas, 8–9
Johnson, Lyndon B., 16–17

Lenin, Vladimir, 11
Lincoln, Abraham, 12–13

McCain, John, 20–21
Mondale, Walter, 25
Muskie, Edmund, 18–19

name-calling, 8, 10, 14, 26
Nixon, Richard, 18

Obama, Barack, 21

Pelosi, Nancy, 23
personal/private information, 14
presidential elections, 8–9, 10, 12–13, 14, 15, 18–19, 20–21, 25, 26–27

racism, 15, 20, 26
Reagan, Ronald, 25
rumor-mongering, 18, 20, 26

Sinclair, Upton, 25
Smith, Gary, 24
Stalin, Joseph, 11
Stevenson, Coke, 16–17

Trump, Donald, 26–27

voting and voting rights, 4–5, 28–29, 30